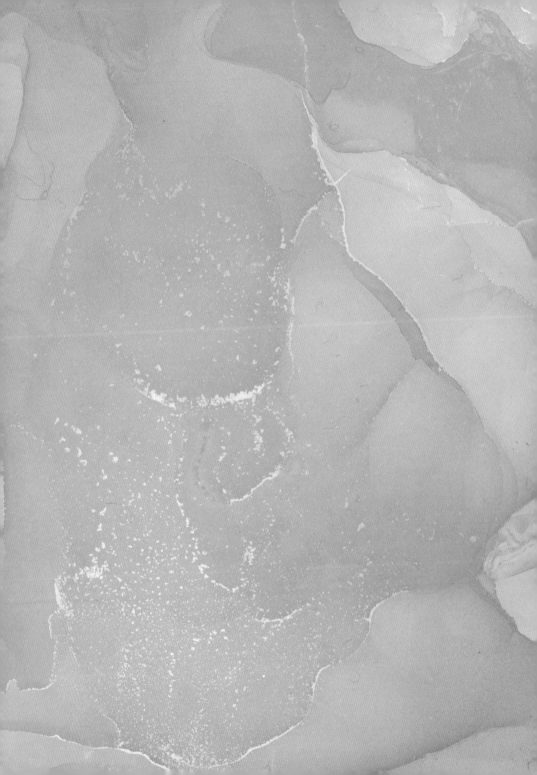

This journal belongs to

....

God already made it plain how to live,
what to do, what God is looking for
in men and women. It's quite simple:
Do what is fair and just to your neighbor,
be compassionate and loyal in your love,
and don't take yourself too seriously—
take God seriously.

MICAH 6:8 MSG

Beauty of Character

To appreciate beauty; to find the best in others; to give one's self;
to leave the world a little better, whether by a healthy child,
a garden patch, or a redeemed social condition; to have played
and laughed with enthusiasm and sung with exultation; to know
even one life has breathed easier because you have lived....
This is to have succeeded.

RALPH WALDO EMERSON

If there is righteousness in the heart, there will be beauty in the
character. If there is beauty in the character there will be
harmony in the home. If there is harmony in the home,
there will be order in the nations. When there is order
in the nations, there will be peace in the world.

CHINESE PROVERB

Peace within makes beauty without.

ENGLISH PROVERB

*Endurance develops strength of character, and character strengthens
our confident hope of salvation. And this hope will not lead to disappointment.
For we know how dearly God loves us.*

ROMANS 5:4–5 NLT

A Place for Dreams

Hold fast your dreams!
Within your heart
Keep one still, secret spot
Where dreams may go
And, sheltered so,
May thrive and grow
Where doubt and fear are not.
O keep a place apart,
Within your heart,
For little dreams to go!

LOUISE DRISCOLL

God created us with an overwhelming desire to soar.
Our desire to develop and use every ounce of potential
He's placed in us is not egotistical. He designed us to be
tremendously productive and "to mount up with wings like eagles,"
realistically dreaming of what He can do with our potential.

CAROL KENT

When dreams come true at last, there is life and joy.
PROVERBS 13:12 TLB

The Majesty of God

Honor and majesty surround him;
strength and beauty fill his sanctuary.

PSALM 96:6 NLT

It was God who first set the stars in space; He is their Maker
and Master—they are all in His hands and subject to His will.
Such are His power and His majesty. Behold your God!

J. I. PACKER

LORD, our LORD, how majestic is your name in all the earth!
You have set your glory in the heavens.... When I consider
your heavens, the work of your fingers, the moon and the stars,
which you have set in place, what is mankind that you are mindful of them,
human beings that you care for them? You have made them a little lower
than the angels and crowned then with glory and honor....
LORD, our LORD, how majestic is your name in all the earth!

PSALM 8:1, 3–5, 9 NIV

The Weaver

My life is but a weaving
Between my Lord and me,
I cannot choose the colors
He worketh steadily.
Oftimes He weaveth sorrow,
And I in foolish pride
Forget He sees the upper
And I, the underside....
The dark threads are as needful
In the Weaver's skillful hand
As the threads of gold and silver
In the pattern He has planned.

GRANT COLFAX TULLER

There are those who suffer greatly, and yet,
through the recognition that pain can be
a thread in the pattern of God's weaving,
find the way to a fundamental joy.

For whatever life holds for you and your family in
the coming days, weave the unfailing fabric of God's
Word through your heart and mind. It will hold
strong, even if the rest of life unravels.

GIGI GRAHAM TCHIVIDJIAN

Blessed are they that mourn:
for they shall be comforted.

MATTHEW 5:4 KJV

Special Plans

This is the real gift: you have been given the breath of life,
designed with a unique, one-of-a-kind soul
that exists forever—the way that you choose to live it
doesn't change the fact that you've been given the gift
of being now and forever. Priceless in value,
you are handcrafted by God, who has a personal design
and plan for each of us. May God's love guide you
through the special plans He has for your life.
Allow your dreams a place in your prayers and plans.
God-given dreams can help you move
into the future He is preparing for you.

The LORD will work out his plans for my life—
for your faithful love, O LORD, endures forever.

PSALM 138:8 NLT

Wonderful Love

Show me the wonders of your great love.... Keep me as the apple
of your eye; hide me in the shadow of your wings.

PSALM 17:7–8 NIV

Give thanks to the LORD, for he is good!
His faithful love endures forever.

PSALM 136:1 NLT

The LORD is merciful and compassionate, slow to get angry
and filled with unfailing love. The LORD is good to everyone.
He showers compassion on all his creation.... The LORD always
keeps his promises; he is gracious in all he does.

PSALM 145: 8–9, 13 NLT

Every one of us as human beings is known and loved by the
Creator apart from every other human on earth.

JAMES DOBSON

Windows of the Soul

Open wide the windows of our spirits and fill us
full of light; open wide the door of our hearts
that we may receive and entertain Thee with
all the powers of our adoration.

CHRISTINA ROSSETTI

Faith goes up the stairs that love has made and looks out
the window which hope has opened.

CHARLES H. SPURGEON

Day-to-day living becomes a window through
which we get a glimpse of life eternal. The eternal
illuminates and gives focus to the daily.

JANICE RIGGLE HUIE

All the earth shall be filled with the glory of the LORD.

NUMBERS 14:21 NKJV

The Love of God

Can anything ever separate us from Christ's love?
Does it mean he no longer loves us if we have trouble
or calamity, or are persecuted, or hungry, or destitute,
or in danger, or threatened with death?... No, despite all
these things, overwhelming victory is ours through Christ,
who loved us. And I am convinced that nothing can ever
separate us from God's love. Neither death nor life, neither
angels nor demons, neither our fears for today nor our
worries about tomorrow—not even the powers of hell
can separate us from God's love. No power in the sky above
or in the earth below—indeed, nothing in all creation
will ever be able to separate us from the love of God
that is revealed in Christ Jesus our Lord.

ROMANS 8:35, 37–39 NLT

Here is the world. Beautiful and terrible
things will happen. Don't be afraid. I am with you.
Nothing can ever separate us.
It's for you I created the universe. I love you.

FREDERICK BUECHNER

Love One Another

Clothe yourselves with compassion, kindness, humility, gentleness and patience. Bear with each other and forgive one another if any of you has a grievance against someone. Forgive as the Lord forgave you. And over all these virtues put on love, which binds them all together in perfect unity.

COLOSSIANS 3:12–14 NIV

Don't just pretend to love others. Really love them. Hate what is wrong. Hold tightly to what is good. Love each other with genuine affection, and take delight in honoring each other.

ROMANS 12:9–10 NLT

May God who gives patience, steadiness, and encouragement help you to live in complete harmony with each other.

ROMANS 15:5 TLB

In God's wisdom, He frequently chooses
to meet our needs by showing His love toward us
through the hands and hearts of others.

JACK HAYFORD

Rest in Him

Truly my soul finds rest in God; my salvation comes from him.
Truly he is my rock and my salvation; he is my fortress,
I will never be shaken…. My salvation and my honor depend on God;
he is my mighty rock, my refuge. Trust in him at all times,
you people; pour out your hearts to him, for God is our refuge….
One thing God has spoken, two things I have heard:
"Power belongs to you, God, and with you, Lord, is unfailing love."

PSALM 62: 1–2, 7–8, 11–12 NIV

Rest in the LORD, and wait patiently for Him.

PSALM 37:7 NKJV

When God finds a soul that rests in Him
and is not easily moved…to this same soul
He gives the joy of His presence.

CATHERINE OF GENOA

The Little Things

It's the little things we do and say
That mean so much as we go our way.
A kindly deed can lift a load
From weary shoulders on the road.
A gentle word, like summer rain,
May soothe some heart and banish pain.
What joy or sadness often springs
From just the simple little things!

WILLA HOEY

Don't ever let yourself get so busy that you miss those little but
important extras in life—the beauty of a day…
the smile of a friend…the serenity of a quiet moment alone.
For it is often life's smallest pleasures and gentlest joys
that make the biggest and most lasting difference.

It's the little things that make up the richest part
of the tapestry of our lives.

*Open your mouth and taste, open your eyes and see—how good GOD is.
Blessed are you who run to him. Worship GOD if you want the best;
worship opens doors to all his goodness.*

PSALM 34:8–9 MSG

God Is Our Refuge

Hear my cry, O God; give heed to my prayer. From the end
of the earth I call to You when my heart is faint; lead me to the rock
that is higher than I. For You have been a refuge for me, a tower
of strength against the enemy. Let me dwell in Your tent forever;
let me take refuge in the shelter of Your wings.

PSALM 61:1–4 NASB

Whom have I in heaven but You? And besides You, I desire nothing
on earth. My flesh and my heart may fail, but God is the strength of
my heart and my portion forever.… As for me, the nearness of God
is my good; I have made the Lord GOD my refuge.

PSALM 73:25–26, 28 NASB

When God has become…our refuge and our fortress,
then we can reach out to Him in the midst of a
broken world and feel at home while still on the way.

HENRI J. M. NOUWEN

Protection

The LORD is my light and my salvation—whom shall I fear?
The LORD is the stronghold of my life—of whom
shall I be afraid?… One thing I ask from the LORD,
this only do I seek: that I may dwell in the house of
the LORD all the days of my life, to gaze on the beauty
of the LORD and to seek him in his temple. For in the
day of trouble he will keep me safe in his dwelling;
he will hide me in the shelter of his sacred tent
and set me high upon a rock…. Hear my voice when I call,
LORD; be merciful to me and answer me. My heart says
of you, "Seek his face!" Your face, LORD, I will seek.

PSALM 27:1, 4–5, 7–8 NIV

Leave behind your fear and dwell on
the lovingkindness of God,
that you may recover by gazing on Him.

God's Thoughts

*How great are your works, LORD,
how profound your thoughts!*

PSALM 92:5 NIV

Just when we least expect it,
[God] intrudes into our neat and tidy notions
about who He is and how He works.

JONI EARECKSON TADA

*The LORD is the everlasting God, the Creator of all the earth.
He never grows weak or weary. No one can measure the depths of
his understanding.… Even youths will become weak and tired,
and young men will fall in exhaustion. But those who trust in the
LORD will find new strength. They will soar high on wings like eagles.
They will run and not grow weary. They will walk and not faint.*

ISAIAH 40:28, 30–31 NLT

Child of God

When we call on God, He bends down His ear to listen,
as a father bends down to listen to his little child.

Elizabeth Charles

He only is the Maker
of all things near and far;
He paints the wayside flower,
He lights the evening star;
the wind and waves obey Him,
by Him the birds are fed;
much more to us, His children,
He gives our daily bread.

Matthias Claudius

Remember you are very special to God as His precious child.
He has promised to complete the good work He has
begun in you. As you continue to grow in Him,
He will make you a blessing to others.

*See what great love the Father has lavished on us, that we
should be called children of God! And that is what we are!*

1 John 3:1 niv

Renewing Word

*You're my place of quiet retreat; I wait for
your Word to renew me.*

PSALM 119:114 MSG

*You have dealt well with Your servant, O LORD, according to
Your word. Teach me good judgment and knowledge,
for I believe in Your commandments. Before I was afflicted
I went astray, but now I keep Your word. You are good,
and do good; teach me Your statutes.*

PSALM 119:65–68 NKJV

*All your words are true; all your
righteous laws are eternal.*

PSALM 119:160 NIV

Full of Laughter

Teach me, Father, to value each day, to live,
to love, to laugh, to play.

KATHI MILLS

Wholehearted, ready laughter heals, encourages, relaxes anyone
within hearing distance. The laughter that springs from love makes
wide the space around it—gives room for the loved one to enter in.
Real laughter welcomes, and never shuts out.

EUGENIA PRICE

Sense of humor; God's great gift
causes spirits to uplift,
Helps to make our bodies mend;
lightens burdens; cheers a friend;
Tickles children; elders grin
at this warmth that glows within;
Surely in the great hereafter
heaven must be full of laughter!

It is often just as sacred to laugh as it is to pray.

CHARLES R. SWINDOLL

*He will yet fill your mouth with laughter
and your lips with shouts of joy.*

JOB 8:21 NIV

Powerful and Faithful

Search high and low, scan skies and land, you'll find nothing and no one quite like GOD. The holy angels are in awe before him; he looms immense and august over everyone around him. GOD-of-the-Angel-Armies, who is like you, powerful and faithful from every angle?

PSALM 89:6–8 MSG

Yours, O LORD, is the greatness, the power, the glory, the victory, and the majesty. Everything in the heavens and on earth is yours, O LORD, and this is your kingdom. We adore you as the one who is over all things.

1 CHRONICLES 29:11 NLT

Ah Lord GOD! Behold, You have made the heavens and the earth by Your great power and by Your outstretched arm! Nothing is too difficult for You.

JEREMIAH 32:17 NASB

Whatever the circumstances, whatever the call…
His strength will be your strength in your hour of need.

BILLY GRAHAM

Treasure in Nature

If we are children of God, we have a tremendous
treasure in nature and will realize that it is holy
and sacred. We will see God reaching out to us in
every wind that blows, every sunrise and sunset,
every cloud in the sky, every flower that blooms,
and every leaf that fades.

OSWALD CHAMBERS

Look up at all the stars in the night sky and hear
your Father saying, "I carefully set each one
in its place. Know that I love you more than these."
Sit by the lake's edge, listening to the water
lapping the shore and hear your Father gently
calling you to that place near His heart.

WENDY MOORE

What a wildly wonderful world, GOD!
You made it all, with Wisdom at your side,
made earth overflow with your wonderful creations.

PSALM 104:24 MSG

I love to think of nature as an unlimited
broadcasting station through which God speaks
to us every hour, if only we will tune in.

GEORGE WASHINGTON CARVER

The Right Word

*Let everything you say be good and helpful, so that your words
will be an encouragement to those who hear them.*

EPHESIANS 4:29 NLT

*Like apples of gold in settings of silver is a word spoken in right
circumstances. Like an earring of gold and an ornament of fine gold
is a wise reprover to a listening ear. Like the cold of snow in the time
of harvest is a faithful messenger to those who send him.*

PROVERBS 25:11–13 NASB

*Whatever you do in word or deed, do all in the name of the
Lord Jesus, giving thanks to God the Father through Him.*

COLOSSIANS 3:17 NKJV

Walk softly. Speak tenderly. Love fervently.

God Draws Near

When you are lonely, I wish you love;
When you are down, I wish you joy;
When you are troubled, I wish you peace;
When things are complicated, I wish you simple beauty;
When things are chaotic, I wish you inner silence;
When things seem empty, I wish you hope,
And the sweet sense of God's presence every passing day.

God still draws near to us in the ordinary,
commonplace, everyday experiences and places....
He comes in surprising ways.

HENRY GARIEPY

In both simple and eloquent ways, our infinite God
personally reveals glimpses of Himself in the finite.

*I have set the LORD always before me; because He is
at my right hand I shall not be moved.*

PSALM 16:8 NKJV

Paths of Life

You have made known to me the paths of life;
You will fill me with joy in your presence.

ACTS 2:28 NIV

But the path of the just is like the shining sun,
that shines ever brighter unto the perfect day.

PROVERBS 4:18 NKJV

Your word is a lamp to my feet and a light to my path.

PSALM 119:105 NASB

Come, and let us go up to the mountain of the LORD….
He will teach us His ways, and we shall walk in His paths.

MICAH 4:2 NKJV

The best things are nearest…light in your eyes,
flowers at your feet, duties at your hand,
the path of God just before you.

ROBERT LOUIS STEVENSON

God's Compassion

Through the LORD's mercies we are not consumed, because His compassions fail not. They are new every morning; great is Your faithfulness. "The LORD is my portion," says my soul, "Therefore I hope in Him!" The LORD is good to those who wait for Him, to the soul who seeks Him.

LAMENTATIONS 3:22–25 NKJV

LORD, don't hold back your tender mercies from me. Let your unfailing love and faithfulness always protect me.

PSALM 40:11 NLT

You, Lord, are a compassionate and gracious God, slow to anger, abounding in love and faithfulness.

PSALM 86:15 NIV

The loving God we serve has immeasurable compassion and tenderness toward each of us throughout our lives.

JAMES DOBSON

Happiness and Gratitude

It is not how much we have, but how much we enjoy,
that makes happiness.

CHARLES H. SPURGEON

Life itself, every bit of health that we enjoy, every hour of liberty
and free enjoyment, the ability to see, to hear, to speak,
to think, and to imagine—all this comes from the hand of God.
We show our gratitude by giving back to Him a part
of that which He has given to us.

BILLY GRAHAM

Our inner happiness depends not on what
we experience but on the degree of
our gratitude to God, whatever the experience.

ALBERT SCHWEITZER

I will bless the LORD at all times;
His praise shall continually be in my mouth.

PSALM 34:1 NKJV

An Undivided Heart

Above all else, guard your heart,
for everything you do flows from it.

PROVERBS 4:23 NIV

I will give them an undivided heart and put a new spirit in them;
I will remove from them their heart of stone and give them a heart
of flesh. Then...they will be my people, and I will be their God.

EZEKIEL 11:19–20 NIV

"Love the LORD your God with all your heart, all your soul,
and all your mind." This is the first and greatest commandment.

MATTHEW 22:37–38 NLT

In the deepest heart of everyone, God planted a longing
for Himself as He is: a God of love.

EUGENIA PRICE

Daily Graces

Thank you, God, for little things
That often come our way,
The things we take for granted
But don't mention when we pray.
The unexpected courtesy,
The thoughtful kindly deed,
A hand reached out to help us
In the time of sudden need.
Oh, make us more aware, dear God,
Of little daily graces
That come to us with sweet surprise
From never-dreamed-of places.

HELEN STEINER RICE

To be grateful is to recognize the love of God in everything
He has given us—and He has given us everything.
Every breath we draw is a gift of His love,
every moment of existence is a gift of grace,
for it brings with it immense graces from Him.

THOMAS MERTON

Give us day by day our daily bread.

LUKE 11:3 NKJV

Seek First

*Look at the birds of the air, that they do not sow, nor reap
nor gather into barns, and yet your heavenly Father feeds them.
Are you not worth much more than they? And who of you by
being worried can add a single hour to his life?
And why are you worried about clothing? Observe how the
lilies of the field grow; they do not toil nor do they spin,
yet I say to you that not even Solomon in all his glory clothed
himself like one of these. But if God so clothes the grass of the field,
which is alive today and tomorrow is thrown into the furnace,
will He not much more clothe you? You of little faith!
Do not worry then, saying, "What will we eat?" or "What will
we drink?" or "What will we wear for clothing?" For…your heavenly
Father knows that you need all these things. But seek first His kingdom
and His righteousness, and all these things will be added to you.*

MATTHEW 6:26–33 NASB

*T*rust the past to the mercy of God, the present to His love,
and the future to His providence.

AUGUSTINE

The Warmth of Love

Though I have seen the oceans and mountains, though I have
read great books and seen great works of art, though I have heard
symphonies and tasted the best wines and foods, there is
nothing greater or more beautiful than those people I love.

CHRISTOPHER DE VINCK

Not every day of our lives is overflowing with joy and celebration.
But there are moments when our hearts nearly burst within us
for the sheer joy of being alive. The first sight of our
newborn babies, the warmth of love in another's eyes,
the fresh scent of rain on a hot summer's eve—moments like
these renew in us a heartfelt appreciation for life.

GWEN ELLIS

When one has once fully entered the realm of love, the world—
no matter how imperfect—becomes rich and beautiful,
for it consists solely of opportunities for love.

SØREN KIERKEGAARD

All of you should be of one mind. Sympathize with each other.
Love each other as brothers and sisters.
Be tenderhearted, and keep a humble attitude.

1 PETER 3:8 NLT

Good Gifts

Every good gift and every perfect gift is from above,
and comes down from the Father of lights,
with whom there is no variation or shadow of turning.

JAMES 1:17 NKJV

Rejoice in the LORD your God! For the rain he sends
demonstrates his faithfulness. Once more the
autumn rains will come, as well as the rains of spring.

JOEL 2:23 NLT

He has not left himself without testimony: He has shown kindness
by giving you rain from heaven and crops in their seasons;
he provides you with plenty of food and fills your hearts with joy.

ACTS 14:17 NIV

All perfect gifts are from above and all our blessings show
The amplitude of God's dear love which any heart may know.

LAURA LEE RANDALL

A Personal Guide

I'll take the hand of those who don't know the way, who can't see where they're going. I'll be a personal guide to them, directing them through unknown country. I'll be right there to show them what roads to take, make sure they don't fall into the ditch. These are the things I'll be doing for them—sticking with them, not leaving them for a minute.

ISAIAH 42:16 MSG

Whether you turn to the right or to the left, your ears will hear a voice behind you, saying, "This is the way; walk in it."

ISAIAH 30:21 NIV

We can make our plans, but the LORD determines our steps.

PROVERBS 16:9 NLT

Heaven often seems distant and unknown,
but if He who made the road…is our guide,
we need not fear to lose the way.

HENRY VAN DYKE

Go Out in Joy

*You'll go out in joy, you'll be led into a whole and complete life.
The mountains and hills will lead the parade, bursting with song. All the
trees of the forest will join the procession, exuberant with applause.*

ISAIAH 55:12 MSG

*You will make known to me the path of life; in Your presence is
fullness of joy; in Your right hand there are pleasures forever.*

PSALM 16:11 NASB

*But let all who take refuge in you rejoice; let them sing joyful
praises forever. Spread your protection over them, that all who
love your name may be filled with joy. For you bless the godly,
O LORD; you surround them with your shield of love.*

PSALM 5:11–12 NLT

Those who run in the path of God's commands
have their hearts set free.

The Rhythms of Life

In waiting we begin to get in touch with the rhythms of life—
stillness and action, listening and decision. They are the
rhythms of God. It is in the everyday and the commonplace
that we learn patience, acceptance, and contentment.

RICHARD J. FOSTER

Love comes while we rest against our Father's chest.
Joy comes when we catch the rhythms of His heart.
Peace comes when we live in harmony with those rhythms.

KEN GIRE

God knows the rhythm of my spirit and knows my heart thoughts.
He is as close as breathing.

How can we honor our God with our lives, the God who gives rain in
both spring and autumn and maintains the rhythm of the seasons?

JEREMIAH 5:24 MSG

Glorious Riches

*I pray that out of his glorious riches he may strengthen
you with power through his Spirit in your inner being,
so that Christ may dwell in your hearts through faith.
And I pray that you, being rooted and established in love,
may have power, together with all the Lord's holy people, to grasp
how wide and long and high and deep is the love of Christ,
and to know this love that surpasses knowledge—that you
may be filled to the measure of all the fullness of God.
Now to him who is able to do immeasurably more than
all we ask or imagine, according to his power that is at work
within us, to him be glory in the church and in Christ Jesus
throughout all generations, for ever and ever! Amen.*

EPHESIANS 3:16–21 NIV

Lord…give me only Your love and Your grace.
With this I am rich enough, and I have no more to ask.

IGNATIUS OF LOYOLA

Life Itself

GOD, your God, will cut away the thick calluses on your heart
and your children's hearts, freeing you to love GOD, your God,
with your whole heart and soul and live, really live....
And you will make a new start, listening obediently to GOD,
keeping all his commandments that I'm commanding you today.
GOD, your God, will outdo himself in making things go well for you....
Love GOD, your God. Walk in his ways. Keep his commandments,
regulations, and rules so that you will live, really live, live exuberantly,
blessed by GOD.... Love GOD, your God, listening obediently
to him, firmly embracing him. Oh yes, he is life itself.

DEUTERONOMY 30:6, 8–9, 16, 20 MSG

I asked God for all things that I might enjoy life.
He gave me life that I might enjoy all things.

An Inner Place

Retire from the world each day to some private spot.... Stay in the secret place till the surrounding noises begin to fade out of your heart and a sense of God's presence envelops you.... Listen for the inward Voice till you learn to recognize it.... Give yourself to God and then be what and who you are without regard to what others think.... Learn to pray inwardly every moment.

A. W. Tozer

The impetus of God's love comes from within Himself, to share with us His life and love. It is a beautiful, eternal gift, held out to us in the hands of love. All we have to do is say "Yes!"

John Powell

I will remember that when I give Him my heart, God chooses to live within me—body and soul. He fills all the empty places, His very Spirit inside of me.

Be beautiful inside, in your hearts, with the lasting charm of a gentle and quiet spirit that is so precious to God.

1 Peter 3:4 TLB

The Grace of God

God, being rich in mercy, because of His great love
with which He loved us, even when we were dead
in our transgressions, made us alive together with
Christ (by grace you have been saved), and raised
us up with Him, and seated us with Him in the
heavenly places in Christ Jesus, so that in the ages
to come He might show the surpassing riches of
His grace in kindness toward us in Christ Jesus.
For by grace you have been saved through faith; and
that not of yourselves, it is the gift of God; not as
a result of works, so that no one may boast. For we
are His workmanship, created in Christ Jesus for
good works, which God prepared beforehand so
that we would walk in them.

EPHESIANS 2:4–10 NASB

Grace means that God already loves us as much
as an infinite God can possibly love.

PHILIP YANCEY

God's Guidance

To You, O LORD, I lift up my soul. O my God, in You I trust, do not let me be ashamed; do not let my enemies exult over me. Indeed, none of those who wait for You will be ashamed.... Make me know Your ways, O LORD; teach me Your paths. Lead me in Your truth and teach me, for You are the God of my salvation; for You I wait all the day. Remember, O LORD, Your compassion and Your lovingkindnesses, for they have been from of old.

PSALM 25:1–6 NASB

God, who has led you safely on so far, will lead you on to the end. Be altogether at rest in the loving holy confidence which you ought to have in His heavenly providence.

FRANCIS DE SALES

A Life Transformed

To pray is to change. This is a great grace. How good of God to provide a path whereby our lives can be taken over by love and joy and peace and patience and kindness and goodness and faithfulness and gentleness and self-control.

RICHARD J. FOSTER

We all, who with unveiled faces contemplate the Lord's glory, are being transformed into his image with ever-increasing glory, which comes from the Lord, who is the Spirit.

2 CORINTHIANS 3:18 NIV

For God is, indeed, a wonderful Father who longs to pour out His mercy upon us, and whose majesty is so great that He can transform us from deep within.

TERESA OF AVILA

Create in me a clean heart, O God; and renew a right spirit within me.

PSALM 51:10 KJV

Love Like That

*Watch what God does, and then you do it,
like children who learn proper behavior from
their parents. Mostly what God does is love you.
Keep company with him and learn a life of love.
Observe how Christ loved us. His love was not
cautious but extravagant. He didn't love in order
to get something from us but to give everything
of himself to us. Love like that.*

EPHESIANS 5:1–2 MSG

Let Jesus be in your heart,
Eternity in your spirit,
The world under your feet,
The will of God in your actions.
And let the love of God shine forth from you.

CATHERINE OF GENOA

*Dear friends, since God so loved us, we also ought
to love one another.... If we love one another,
God lives in us and his love is made complete in us.*

1 JOHN 4:11–12 NIV

By Love Alone

By love alone is God enjoyed; by love alone
delighted in, by love alone approached and admired.
His nature requires love.

THOMAS TRAHERNE

There is an essential connection between
experiencing God, loving God, and trusting God.
You will trust God only as much as you love Him,
and you will love Him to the extent you have
touched Him, rather that He has touched you.

BRENNAN MANNING

Although it be good to think upon the kindness of
God, and to love Him and worship Him for it; yet
it is far better to gaze upon the pure essence of Him
and to love Him and worship Him for Himself.

Trust God's Heart

He writes in characters too grand
for our short sight to understand.
We catch but broken strokes
and try to fathom all the withered hopes
Of death, of life,
the endless war, the useless strife....
But there, with larger, clearer sight, we shall see this:
His way was right.

JOHN OXENHAM

Trust God where you cannot trace Him.
Do not try to penetrate the cloud He brings
over you; rather look to the bow that is on it.
The mystery is God's; the promise is yours.

JOHN MACDUFF

Wait upon God's strengthening, and say to Him,
"O Lord, You have been our refuge in all
generations." Trust in Him who has placed this
burden on you. What you yourself cannot bear,
bear with the help of God who is all-powerful.

BONIFACE

Your Personal God

Don't be afraid, I've redeemed you.
I've called your name. You're mine.
When you're in over your head,
I'll be there with you.
When you're in rough waters,
you will not go down.
When you're between a rock and a hard place,
it won't be a dead end—
Because I am God, your personal God,
The Holy of Israel, your Savior.
I paid a huge price for you…!
That's how much you mean to me!
That's how much I love you!

ISAIAH 43:1–4 MSG

Do not be afraid to enter the cloud that
is settling down on your life. God is in it.
The other side is radiant with His glory.

L. B. COWMAN

Let the one who walks in the dark,
who has no light,
trust in the name of the LORD
and rely on their God.

ISAIAH 50:10 NIV

Always There

We need never shout across the spaces to
an absent God. He is nearer than our own soul,
closer than our most secret thoughts.

A. W. TOZER

God is the sunshine that warms us, the rain
that melts the frost and waters the young plants.
The presence of God is a climate of strong and
bracing love, always there.

JOAN ARNOLD

God is always present in the temple of your heart...
His home. And when you come in to meet Him
there, you find that it is the one place of deep
satisfaction where every longing is met.

Always be in a state of expectancy, and see that you
leave room for God to come in as He likes.

OSWALD CHAMBERS

A living, loving God can and does make His
presence felt, can and does speak to us in the silence
of our hearts, can and does warm and caress us till
we no longer doubt that He is near, that He is here.

BRENNAN MANNING

An Invitation

Come, all you who are thirsty,
come to the waters; and you who
have no money, come, buy and eat!
Come, buy wine and milk
without money and without cost.
Why spend money on what is not bread,
and your labor on what does not satisfy?
Listen, listen to me, and eat what is good,
and you will delight in the richest of fare.
Give ear and come to me;
listen, that you may live.

ISAIAH 55:1–3 NIV

God is looking for people who will come
in simple dependence upon His grace,
and rest in simple faith upon His greatness.
At this very moment, He's looking at you.

JACK HAYFORD

Are you tired? Worn out? Burned out on religion?
Come to me. Get away with me and
you'll recover your life. I'll show you how
to take a real rest. Walk with me and work
with me—watch how I do it. Learn the unforced
rhythms of grace. I won't lay anything heavy
or ill-fitting on you. Keep company with me
and you'll learn to live freely and lightly.

MATTHEW 11:28–30 MSG

A Safe Journey

He rescues you from hidden traps,
shields you from deadly hazards.
His huge outstretched arms protect you—
under them you're perfectly safe;
his arms fend off all harm.
Fear nothing—not wild wolves in the night,
not flying arrows in the day,
not disease that prowls through the darkness,
not disaster that erupts at high noon....
"If you'll hold on to me for dear life," says GOD,
"I'll get you out of any trouble.
I'll give you the best of care
if you'll only get to know and trust me.
Call me and I'll answer, be at your side
in bad times."

PSALM 91:3–6, 14–15 MSG

May your life become one of glad
and unending praise to the Lord as you
journey through this world.

TERESA OF AVILA

God has not promised us an easy journey,
but He has promised us a safe journey.

WILLIAM C. MILLER

Nothing But Grace

There is nothing but God's grace. We walk
upon it; we breathe it; we live and die by it;
it makes the nails and axles of the universe.

ROBERT LOUIS STEVENSON

The "air" which our souls need also envelops
all of us at all times and on all sides. God
is round about us in Christ on every hand,
with many-sided and all-sufficient grace.
All we need to do is to open our hearts.

OLE HALLESBY

Jesus Christ opens wide the doors of the treasure
house of God's promises, and bids us go in and
take with boldness the riches that are ours.

CORRIE TEN BOOM

GOD is sheer mercy and grace;
not easily angered, he's rich in love.

PSALM 103:8 MSG

He Carries Our Sorrows

There is a sacredness in tears.
They are not the mark of weakness,
but of power. They speak more eloquently
than ten thousand tongues. They are
the messengers of overwhelming grief,
of deep contrition, and of unspeakable love.

WASHINGTON IRVING

Your tears are precious to God. They are like
stained-glass windows in the darkness, whose true
beauty is revealed only when there is a light within.

When Jesus…confides to us that
He is "acquainted with Grief,"
we listen, for that also is an
Acquaintance of our own.

EMILY DICKINSON

Surely He has borne our griefs
and carried our sorrows….
By His stripes we are healed.

ISAIAH 53:4–5 NKJV

Showers of Blessings

*Bless the LORD, O my soul;
And all that is within me, bless His holy name!
Bless the LORD, O my soul,
And forget not all His benefits:
Who forgives all your iniquities,
Who heals all your diseases,
Who redeems your life from destruction,
Who crowns you with lovingkindness
and tender mercies,
Who satisfies your mouth with good things,
So that your youth is renewed like the eagle's.*

PSALM 103:1–5 NKJV

God, who is love—who is, if I may say it this way,
made out of love—simply cannot help but shed
blessing on blessing upon us.

HANNAH WHITALL SMITH

God is waiting for us to come to Him with our
needs…. God's throne room is always open….
Every single believer in the whole world could
walk into the throne room all at one time,
and it would not even be crowded.

CHARLES STANLEY

Comfort Sweet

He is the Source. Of everything.
Strength for your day. Wisdom for your task.
Comfort for your soul. Grace for your battle.
Provision for each need.

JACK HAYFORD

There is a place of comfort sweet
Near to the heart of God;
A place where we our Savior meet,
Near to the heart of God.
O Jesus, blest Redeemer....
Hold us who wait before Thee
Near to the heart of God.

CLELAND B. MCAFEE

God comforts. He lays His right hand on the
wounded soul...and He says, as if that one were
the only soul in all the universe: O greatly beloved,
fear not: peace be unto thee.

AMY CARMICHAEL

Every now and again take a good look at
something not made with hands—a mountain,
a star, the turn of a stream. There will come to you
wisdom and patience and solace and, above all,
the assurance that you are not alone in the world.

SIDNEY LOVETT

Seek the Lord

In extravagance of soul, we seek His face.
In generosity of heart, we glean His gentle touch.
In excessiveness of spirit, we love Him, and
His love comes back to us a hundredfold.

TRICIA MCCARY RHODES

*The God who made the world and everything in it
is the Lord of heaven and earth…. He himself gives
everyone life and breath and everything else….
God did this so that they would seek him and
perhaps reach out for him and find him, though
he is not far from any one of us. "For in him
we live, and move, and have our being."*

ACTS 17:24–25, 27–28 NIV

I have sought Thy nearness;
With all my heart have I called Thee,
And going out to meet Thee
I found Thee coming toward me.

YEHUDA HALEVI

Faithful Guide

Guidance is a sovereign act. Not merely does God
will to guide us by showing us His way...whatever
mistakes we may make, we shall come safely home.
Slippings and strayings there will be, no doubt, but
the everlasting arms are beneath us; we shall be
caught, rescued, restored. This is God's promise;
this is how good He is. And our self-distrust, while
keeping us humble, must not cloud the joy with
which we lean on our faithful covenant God.

J. I. PACKER

Heaven often seems distant and unknown,
but if he who made the road...is our guide,
we need not fear to lose the way.

HENRY VAN DYKE

When we obey him, every path he
guides us on is fragrant with his
loving-kindness and his truth.

PSALM 25:10 TLB

Settled in Solitude

Solitude liberates us from entanglements by carving
out a space from which we can see ourselves and
our situation before the Audience of One. Solitude
provides the private place where we can take our
bearings and so make God our North Star.

Os Guinness

We must drink deeply from the very Source the
deep calm and peace of interior quietude and
refreshment of God, allowing the pure water of
divine grace to flow plentifully and unceasingly
from the Source itself.

Mother Teresa

*Whoever drinks of the water that I will give
him shall never thirst; but the water that
I will give him will become in him a well
of water springing up to eternal life.*

John 4:14 NASB

Settle yourself in solitude and you will
come upon Him in yourself.

Teresa of Avila

God Understands

He heals the brokenhearted
and binds up their wounds.
He determines the number of the stars
and calls them each by name.
Great is our Lord and mighty in power;
his understanding has no limit....
The LORD delights in those who fear him,
who put their hope in his unfailing love.

PSALM 147:3–5, 11 NIV

God understands our prayers even when
we can't find the words to say them.

God possesses infinite knowledge and an awareness
which is uniquely His. At all times, even in the
midst of any type of suffering, I can realize that
He knows, loves, watches, understands,
and more than that, He has a purpose.

BILLY GRAHAM

Trust in the LORD with all your heart;
And lean not on your own understanding;
In all your ways acknowledge Him,
And He shall direct your paths.

PROVERBS 3:5–6 NKJV

New Every Morning

Experience God in the breathless wonder and
startling beauty that is all around you. His sun
shines warm upon your face. His wind whispers in
the treetops. Like the first rays of morning light,
celebrate the start of each day with God.

WENDY MOORE

Those who have met God are not looking
for something—they have found it;
they are not searching for light—upon them
the Light has already shined.

A. W. TOZER

Always new. Always exciting. Always full of
promise. The mornings of our lives,
each a personal daily miracle!

GLORIA GAITHER

A quiet morning with a loving God puts the events
of the upcoming day into proper perspective.

JANETTE OKE

Sweet Hour of Prayer

Sweet hour of prayer, sweet hour of prayer,
That calls me from a world of care,
And bids me at my Father's throne,
Make all my wants and wishes known!
In seasons of distress and grief,
My soul has often found relief,
And oft escaped the tempter's snare
By thy return, sweet hour of prayer.

WILLIAM W. WALFORD

If we knew how to listen, we would hear Him
speaking to us. For God does speak…. If we knew
how to listen to God, if we knew how to look
around us, our whole life would become prayer.

MICHAEL QUOIST

All good meditative prayer is a conversion
of our entire self to God.

THOMAS MERTON

*I call on you, my God, for you will answer me;
turn your ear to me and hear my prayer.*

PSALM 17:6 NIV

Totally Aware

God is every moment totally aware of each
one of us. Totally aware in intense
concentration and love…. No one passes
through any area of life, happy or tragic,
without the attention of God with him.

EUGENIA PRICE

Because God is responsible for our welfare,
we are told to cast all our care upon Him,
for He cares for us. God says, "I'll take the burden—
don't give it a thought—leave it to Me."
God is keenly aware that we are dependent
upon Him for life's necessities.

BILLY GRAHAM

You are God's created beauty and the focus
of His affection and delight.

JANET L. WEAVER SMITH

Take Refuge

Let my soul take refuge…beneath the shadow
of Your wings: let my heart, this sea of restless
waves, find peace in You, O God.

AUGUSTINE

My Good Shepherd, who have shown Your very
gentle mercy to us,…give grace and strength to me,
Your little lamb, that in no tribulation or anguish
or pain may I turn away from You.

FRANCIS OF ASSISI

God stands fast as your rock, steadfast
as your safeguard, sleepless as your watcher,
valiant as your champion.

CHARLES H. SPURGEON

As for God, his way is perfect….
He shields all who take refuge in him.

PSALM 18:30 NIV

The LORD is good,
a refuge in times of trouble.
He cares for those who trust in him.

NAHUM 1:7 NIV

That I May Know Him

*I want you woven into a tapestry of love,
in touch with everything there is to know of God.
Then you will have minds confident and at rest,
focused on Christ, God's great mystery. All the
richest treasures of wisdom and knowledge are
embedded in that mystery and nowhere else.*

COLOSSIANS 2:2–3 MSG

He is a God who can be found. A God who
can be known. A God who wants to be close to us.
That's why He is called Immanuel,
which means "God with us." But He draws
close to us as we draw close to Him.

STORMIE OMARTIAN

Give us, Lord: a pure heart that we may
see Thee, a humble heart that we may
hear Thee, a heart of love that we may serve
Thee, a heart of faith that we may live with Thee.

DAG HAMMARSKJÖLD

The God of All Comfort

We may ask, "Why does God bring thunderclouds
and disasters when we want green pastures
and still waters?" Bit by bit, we find behind the
clouds, the Father's feet; behind the lightning,
an abiding day that has no night; behind the
thunder, a still small voice that comforts
with a comfort that is unspeakable.

OSWALD CHAMBERS

I look behind me and you're there,
then up ahead and you're there, too—
your reassuring presence, coming and going.
This is too much, too wonderful—
I can't take it all in!

PSALM 139:5–6 MSG

God walks with us…. He scoops us up in His arms
or simply sits with us in silent strength until we
cannot avoid the awesome recognition that yes,
even now, He is here.

GLORIA GAITHER

The LORD is near to the brokenhearted
And saves those who are crushed in spirit.

PSALM 34:18 NASB

Delight in the Lord

Take delight in the LORD,
and he will give you the desires of your heart.
Commit your way to the LORD;
trust in him and he will do this:
He will make your righteous reward shine
like the dawn, your vindication like the noonday sun.

PSALM 37:4–6 NIV

Send me your light and your faithful care,
let them lead me; let them
bring me to your holy mountain,
to the place where you dwell.
Then will I go to the altar of God,
to God, my joy and my delight.

PSALM 43:3–4 NIV

I delight to do Your will, O my God,
And Your law is within my heart.

PSALM 40:8 NKJV

God's Answers

A wise gardener plants his seeds,
then has the good sense not to dig them up
every few days to see if a crop is on the way.
Likewise, we must be patient as God
brings the answers…in His own good time.

QUIN SHERRER

Being able to bow in prayer as the day begins or
ends gives expression to the frustrations
and concerns that might not otherwise
be ventilated. On the other end of that prayer
line is a loving heavenly Father who has promised
to hear and answer our petitions.

JAMES DOBSON

We shall come one day to a heaven where we shall
gratefully know that God's great refusals were
sometimes the true answers to our truest prayer.

P. T. FORSYTH

Now I know in part, but then I will know
fully just as I also have been fully known.

1 CORINTHIANS 13:12 NASB

Fresh Hope

I don't know, when I'm asking for something
here on earth, what is going on in the innermost
shrine of Heaven (I like to think about it, though).
I am sure of one thing: it is good. Because Jesus
is there. Jesus loves me. Jesus has gone into
that shrine on my behalf. The hope we have
is a living hope, an unassailable one.
We wait for it, in faith and patience.

ELISABETH ELLIOT

GOD...rekindles burned-out lives with fresh hope,
restoring dignity and respect to their lives—
a place in the sun! For the very structures
of earth are GOD's; he has laid out
his operations on a firm foundation.

1 SAMUEL 2:7–8 MSG

Within each of us, just waiting to blossom,
is the wonderful promise of all we can be.

Let your unfailing love surround us, LORD,
for our hope is in you alone.

PSALM 33:22 NLT

Sought and Found

It is God's will that we believe that we see Him
continually, though it seems to us that the sight be
only partial; and through this belief He makes us
always to gain more grace, for God wishes to be
seen, and He wishes to be sought, and He wishes
to be expected, and He wishes to be trusted.

JULIAN OF NORWICH

If you are seeking after God, you may be sure
of this: God is seeking you much more.
He is the Lover, and you are His beloved.
He has promised Himself to you.

JOHN OF THE CROSS

They who seek the throne of grace
Find that throne in every place;
If we live a life of prayer,
God is present everywhere.

OLIVER HOLDEN

Seek the LORD your God, you
will find him if you seek him with all
your heart and with all your soul.

DEUTERONOMY 4:29 NIV

Praise Overflows

All enjoyment spontaneously overflows into praise....
The world rings with praise.... I think we delight to praise what
we enjoy because the praise not merely expresses but completes
the enjoyment; it is the appointed consummation.

C. S. Lewis

Does not all nature around me praise God?
If I were silent, I should be an exception to the universe.
Does not the thunder praise Him as it rolls like
drums in the march of the God of armies?...
Does not the lightning write His name in letters of fire?
Has not the whole earth a voice? And...can I silent be?

Charles H. Spurgeon

God's pursuit of praise from us and our pursuit of pleasure
in Him are one and the same pursuit. God's quest
to be glorified and our quest to be satisfied reach
their goal in this one experience: our delight in
God which overflows in praise.

John Piper

Oh, sing to the LORD a new song! Sing to the LORD, all the earth.

Psalm 96:1 NKJV

Countless Beauties

From the world we see, hear, and touch, we behold inspired
visions that reveal God's glory. In the sun's light, we catch
warm rays of grace and glimpse His eternal design.
In the birds' song, we hear His voice and it reawakens
our desire for Him. At the wind's touch,
we feel His Spirit and sense our eternal existence.

WENDY MOORE

May God give you eyes to see beauty
only the heart can understand.

It is one of the beautiful compensations of this life
that no person can sincerely try to help
another without helping himself.

RALPH WALDO EMERSON

All the world is an utterance of the Almighty.
Its countless beauties, its exquisite adaptations,
all speak to you of Him.

PHILLIPS BROOKS

Oh, worship the LORD in the beauty of holiness!

PSALM 96:9 NKJV

At Home in His Love

*Make your home in me just as I do in you. In the same way
that a branch can't bear grapes by itself but only by being joined
to the vine, you can't bear fruit unless you are joined with me.
I am the Vine, you are the branches. When you're joined with me
and I with you, the relation intimate and organic, the harvest is sure
to be abundant. Separated, you can't produce a thing....
But if you make yourselves at home with me and my words are
at home in you, you can be sure that whatever you ask will
be listened to and acted upon.... I've loved you the way my Father
has loved me. Make yourselves at home in my love.*

JOHN 15:4–9 MSG

This is and has been the Father's work
from the beginning—
to bring us into the home of His heart.

GEORGE MACDONALD

To Be Alive

It seems to me we can never give up
longing and wishing while we are alive.
There are certain things
we feel to be beautiful and good,
and we must hunger for them.

GEORGE ELIOT

It is the simple things of life that make living worthwhile,
the sweet fundamental things such as love and duty,
work and rest, and living close to nature.

LAURA INGALLS WILDER

The LORD will command His lovingkindness in the daytime;
and His song will be with me in the night,
a prayer to the God of my life.

PSALM 42:8 NASB

Indescribable Love

Could we with ink the ocean fill,
And were the skies of parchment made;
Were every stalk on earth a quill,
And every man a scribe by trade;
To write the love of God above
Would drain the ocean dry;
Nor could the scroll contain the whole,
Though stretched from sky to sky.

MEIR BEN ISAAC NEHORAI

Love is the response of the heart
to the overwhelming goodness of God....
You may be so awestruck and full of love
at His presence that words do not come.

RICHARD J. FOSTER

Thanks be to God for His indescribable gift!

2 CORINTHIANS 9:15 NASB

Abundant Life

*I came so they can have real and eternal life,
more and better life than they ever dreamed of.*

JOHN 10:10 MSG

*In the beginning was the Word, and the Word was with God,
and the Word was God. He was in the beginning with God.
All things came into being through Him, and apart from
Him nothing came into being that has come into being.
In Him was life, and the life was the Light of men....
For of His fullness we have all received, and grace upon grace.*

JOHN 1:1–4, 16 NASB

He is looking for people who will come in
simple dependence upon His grace....
At this very moment, He's looking at you.

JACK HAYFORD

Glorious Handiwork

He made you so you could share in His creation,
could love and laugh and know Him.

TED GRIFFEN

You are a creation of God unequaled anywhere
in the universe.... Thank Him for yourself and then
for all the rest of His glorious handiwork.

NORMAN VINCENT PEALE

The huge dome of the sky is of all things sensuously
perceived the most like infinity. When God made space
and worlds that move in space, and clothed our world
with air, and gave us such eyes and such imaginations as
those we have, He knew what the sky would mean to us....
We cannot be certain that this was not indeed one
of the chief purposes for which Nature was created.

C. S. LEWIS

The heavens declare His righteousness,
and all the peoples see His glory.

PSALM 97:6 NKJV

Watchful Care

God takes care of His own. He knows our needs.
He anticipates our crises. He is moved by our weaknesses.
He stands ready to come to our rescue. And at just
the right moment, He steps in and proves Himself
as our faithful heavenly Father.

CHARLES R. SWINDOLL

He paints the lily of the field,
Perfumes each lily bell;
If He so loves the little flowers,
I know He loves me well.

MARIA STRAUS

God cares for the world He created, from the rising
of a nation to the falling of the sparrow.
Everything in the world lies under the watchful gaze
of His providential eyes, from the numbering of the days
of our life to the numbering of the hairs on our head.

KEN GIRE

For He will give His angels charge concerning you,
to guard you in all your ways.

PSALM 91:11 NASB

The Miracle of Friendship

There's a miracle called friendship
That dwells within the heart,
And you don't know how it happens
Or where it gets its start.
But the happiness it brings you
Always gives a special lift,
And you realize that friendship
Is life's most precious gift.

The first blush of friendship is a grace to behold:
a moment of shyness, a tentative hello.
Every other gift in life takes wing from here—
affection, generosity, sharing—until soon your life is rich.

The impulse of love that leads us to the doorway
of a friend is the voice of God within.

AGNES SANFORD

A friend loves at all times.
PROVERBS 17:17 NKJV

Faith Is the Centerpiece

Faith does more than give reality to that which we do not see;
it makes us look differently at visible things…. Faith, as the Bible
defines it, is present-tense action. Faith means being sure of
what we hope for…now. It means knowing something is real,
this moment, all around you, even when you don't see it.
Great faith isn't the ability to believe long and far
into the misty future. It's simply taking God
at His word and taking the next step.

JONI EARECKSON TADA

Faith is the centerpiece of a connected life.
It allows us to live by the grace of invisible strands.
It is a belief in a wisdom superior to our own.

TERRY TEMPEST WILLIAMS

*Because of Christ and our faith in him, we can now
come boldly and confidently into God's presence.*

EPHESIANS 3:12 NLT

The Garden of My Life

*At that same time, a fine vineyard will appear. There's something
to sing about! I, GOD, tend it. I keep it well-watered. I keep careful
watch over it so that no one can damage it…. Even if it gives me thistles
and thornbushes, I'll just pull them out and burn them up. Let that
vine cling to me for safety, let it find a good and whole life with me,
let it hold on for a good and whole life.*

ISAIAH 27:2–5 MSG

*The LORD will guide you always; he will satisfy your needs
in a sun-scorched land and will strengthen your frame.
You will be like a well-watered garden,
like a spring whose waters never fail.*

ISAIAH 58:11 NIV

It is God's knowledge of me, His careful husbanding of
the ground of my being, His constant presence in the garden
of my little life that guarantees my joy.

W. PHILLIP KELLER

Designed on Purpose

*All the days ordained for me were written in
your book before one of them came to be.*

PSALM 139:16 NIV

*It's in Christ that we find out who we are and what we are living for.
Long before we first heard of Christ and got our hopes up, he had
his eye on us, had designs on us for glorious living, part of the
overall purpose he is working out in everything and everyone.*

EPHESIANS 1:11–12 MSG

*To everything there is a season, a time for
every purpose under heaven.*

ECCLESIASTES 3:1 NKJV

*The plans of the LORD stand firm forever, the purposes
of his heart through all generations.*

PSALM 33:11 NIV

*The patterns of our days are always rearranging…
and each design for living is unique,
graced with its own special beauty.*

Made for Joy

Our hearts were made for joy. Our hearts were made to enjoy the One who created them. Too deeply planted to be much affected by the ups and downs of life, this joy is a knowing and a being known by our Creator. He sets our hearts alight with radiant joy.

If one is joyful, it means that one is faithfully living for God, and that nothing else counts; and if one gives joy to others, one is doing God's work. With joy without and joy within, all is well.

JANET ERSKINE STUART

Live for today but hold your hands open to tomorrow. Anticipate the future and its changes with joy. There is a seed of God's love in every event, every circumstance, every unpleasant situation in which you may find yourself.

BARBARA JOHNSON

The joy of the LORD is your strength.

NEHEMIAH 8:10 NKJV

The Beauty of Dreams

We grow great by dreams…. [We] see things in the soft haze
of a spring day or in the red fire of a long winter's evening.
Some of us let these great dreams die, but others nourish and
protect them; nurse them through bad days till they bring them
to the sunshine and light, which comes always to those who
sincerely hope that their dreams will come true.

WOODROW WILSON

The future belongs to those who believe
in the beauty of their dreams.

ELEANOR ROOSEVELT

God gives us dreams so we'll long for His reality.

BETH MOORE

Trust steadily in God, hope unswervingly, love extravagantly.

1 CORINTHIANS 13:13 MSG

Hope in God

Why are you in despair, O my soul?
And why have you become disturbed within me?
Hope in God, for I shall again praise Him
For the help of His presence.
O my God, my soul is in despair within me;
Therefore I remember You....
Deep calls to deep at the sound of Your waterfalls;
All Your breakers and Your waves have
rolled over me.
The LORD will command His lovingkindness
in the daytime;
And His song will be with me in the night,
A prayer to the God of my life.

PSALM 42:5–8 NASB

Let all that I am wait quietly before God,
for my hope is in him.

PSALM 62:5 NLT